FORD END

THE STORY OF AN ESSEX VILLAGE

by
WINIFRED EASTMENT

"*The web of our life is of a mingled yarn; good and ill together.*"

SHAKESPEARE.

Published by
ESSEX COUNTRYSIDE
Letchworth Printers Limited
Norton Way North
Letchworth, Hertfordshire

Printed by Letchworth Printers Ltd., Norton Way North, Letchworth

FORD END
THE STORY OF AN ESSEX VILLAGE

CONTENTS

ILLUSTRATIONS

FOREWORD TO THE NEW EDITION

IN the natural order of things *nothing* is static, so whether we like it or not we all have to accept the element of change as a normal condition of life.

Even the so-called "somnolent" little villages and hamlets, relatively becalmed in the yet unspoilt backwaters of a revolutionary age (and fortunate, indeed, still to be enjoying the peace and quiet and natural beauty of their surroundings!), are not exempt from this inexorable law of change, only being farther from the hub of restless activity the process is slower, and therefore less noticeable.

All the same, much can happen in a decade to render a village history somewhat outdated, at least in its minor aspects. In ten years properties change hands; ambitious conversions disguise and distort original features; period houses disappear to make way for mushroom growths on contemporary lines; available sites get eagerly snapped up and centuries-old trees and cherished landmarks are sacrificed in the interests of speculative building; death takes its toll and familiar faces and valued old friends are missed, but the stork remains busy, delivering new arrivals to restore the balance; yesterday's schoolchildren join the ranks of today's wage-earners, encounter romance and embark on matrimony; the hard-working middle-aged sector begins seriously to plan for retirement; age-old customs surrender to "trendy" influences; traditional local interests cease to attract; and once-popular organizations suffer declining support and the prospect of eventual shut-down. In short, it all adds up to a slow, relentless transformation.

It was in 1958 that this village chronicle was first

published, and in the meantime Ford End has inevitably experienced most of the symptoms of this gradual metamorphosis. Many of the well-known characters have passed on and others have moved away; dwellings have been bought, sold, restored and extended, and new ones have been built. The mellow, weatherboarded cottages in The Chase—owned by the late Mr. and Mrs. J. Wilks—have been skilfully converted into a single sizeable residence and given a complete face-lift. The old allotment field is now the site of Russetts, a substantial bungalow whose pleasant garden already presents the illusion of maturity. The school has been enlarged and has acquired its own well-equipped canteen, and the village hall has suffered a corresponding decline in bookings. In several instances farms are now being carried on by the next generation—former "young farmers" who have graduated in the school of practical experience to administrative status. Certain of the local organizations, including, surprisingly, the Women's Institute and the Garden Association, have ceased to function (at least temporarily). The spacious vicarage, unoccupied since 1966, is up for sale*; but, significantly, the extension to the churchyard acquired in the early 1950s has now been brought into use. There have been new acquisitions in church furnishing, notably the green altar frontal given by her family in memory of the late Mrs. Alice Burr and dedicated on April 28, 1968. The recent theft of the church brass, including candlesticks, vases and the alms dish, caused natural consternation, but its early recovery—thanks to the alertness of the police—aroused corresponding jubilation.

Thus the passage of time has left its dents and scars on the old surface, but the basic structure stands foursquare and is likely to expand.

The reader, then, noting any apparent discrepancies

* *Stop press.* Its withdrawal is now likely.

between the text and the current situation is asked to make allowance for the intervening ten years.

In 1970 the parish of Ford End will celebrate its centenary, and this will mark a really important milestone in its history; it could be an occasion for reappraisal.

What, then, of the future? Who dares to predict? We may dream wistful dreams, indulge in idle speculation, entertain extravagant hopes, draw up impressive blueprints and be rash enough to bank on the outcome, crystal gaze with fixed intent and prophesy endlessly and daringly, but history alone will provide the answer. What can, however, be reasonably assumed is that as it enters its second century Ford End will draw inspiration from the past and step with boldness and imagination into the future; it could be that the centennial year will usher in a resurgence of village life in all aspects, spiritual and secular.

WINIFRED EASTMENT.

Wanstead. July 1968.

CHAPTER 1

THE VILLAGE SCENE

HISTORICALLY speaking it could be said that the village of Ford End has not yet reached adolescence and that the presentation of a village history at this stage is rather like the autobiography of a precocious seven-year-old. History, however, is not concerned only with the shadowy events of a receding past. It is a *living* thing, registering current and continuous processes; building today, on yesterday's experiences, for tomorrow. So as an up-and-coming community Ford End is in course of amassing its historical wealth. The present brief record is an attempt to assess its fortune to date, and to invest it for posterity.

Ford End, according to reliable old records and maps (such as Morant's *History and Antiquities of the County of Essex* and Chapman and André's map of 1777), was originally known as Fourth End. It was formerly one of the eight small hamlets comprising the parish of Great Waltham, having no independent status until 1870. Even then the independence acquired was only partial: it became a separate ecclesiastical parish, remaining for purposes of local government an integral part of Great Waltham, on whose parish council two local representatives sit.

Agreement seems to be lacking as to why and when Fourth End became Ford End, but a likely clue is supposed to be the ford over the brook at the foot of Sandon Hill. The postal authorities became the final arbiters in favour of the modern version—no doubt with good reason, for one can well imagine that the concurrent usage of both names must have been very confusing.

Ford End is an agreeably attractive, somnolent little village in the heart of rural Essex, eight miles from Chelmsford and four from Dunmow, with the Roothings (or Rodings) and Easters as near neighbours. It has no railway and only an infrequent bus service. It enjoys a healthy altitude of 225 feet above sea level at the village centre.

The main Chelmsford—Dunmow road follows a truly serpentine course through the village, and being both undulating and tortuous the local scene is absolved from any charge of monotony. The steep hill which forms the main highway through the village seems to withstand the weight of modern traffic remarkably well, but formerly it was little more than a narrow cart track. During the past seventy years the roads have improved beyond recognition, and two outstanding improvements involved the modification of sharp, dangerous corners at Appletrees and The Turning. Only within the last year or so have the side lanes and turnings been officially named—to facilitate postal deliveries.

From the extreme northerly point of Absol Park right down to Hartford End—where the road crosses it—the River Chelmer provides a natural, winding boundary between the two parishes of Ford End and Felsted; thence it pursues a leisurely course towards Chelmsford across the eastern end of the parish, skirting Littley Green. In the vicinity of the mill the river presents a strikingly lovely picture, with the graceful willows and pleasant garden of the Mill House contributing handsomely to the natural surrounding beauty. The Mill House itself, like a jewel in a perfect setting, can never fail to cast its spell over the wayfarer approaching for the first time, especially if that time is in early summer when the mellowed brick wall is richly festooned with wistaria. This part of the river is the recognized bathing site, and is well patronized in season.

Ford End's population of under 1,000 is unevenly distributed, the village centre claiming about half and the rest being scattered indiscriminately over the remoter parts —Littley Green, Hartford End, North End, Rolphy Green.

The variable soil, with clay subsoil, provides excellent arable land for the farms that offer the main source of local employment. The old clay-pit was filled in to make way for the first batch of council houses. The clay had been excavated to improve the condition of surrounding fields. It is claimed that up to 1912 agriculture absorbed almost the entire local labour; nobody worked outside the village and most of those who were not on the land were employed at the Hartford End brewery. But after World War I a drift from the land set in. The introduction of public transport into the countryside accelerated the drift, especially towards the large factories in Chelmsford. The lure of high wages in office and factory added momentum, and the mechanization of agriculture may have played its part too.

The existence of osier beds in the district accounted for a small local industry and also, according to the school log book of the 1870s, for wholesale absenteeism among the scholars. Entries record, for instance, " May 8th, absence as children away osier peeling "; " May 15th, osier peeling; poor attendance "; " June 12th, osier peeling finished." These tell their own tale. The osier beds were close to the school, and the temptation to earn a few coppers in days when money was all too scarce must have been hard to resist. The bunglalow—Willowcot—opposite the church was built by three brothers named Coe—Josiah, Jeremiah and Obadiah. This site comprised part of the osier beds, and the enterprising Coe family ran a small basket-making industry. The date of their undertaking is unconfirmed, but it was certainly before 1870, when the church was built.

The main features of the village conform pleasantly to rustic tradition, with the parish church (St. John the Evangelist), the school, the cricket green, the village hall and the Spreadeagle inn all within a stone's throw of each other and providing a compelling focal point. The fine cricket field ensures a restful outlook for the surrounding cottages, and their grandstand view of the season's matches is something to be envied.

In addition to the larger farmhouses and the typical little cottages belonging to them, Ford End has its share of enchanting old-world thatched dwellings—in some cases clever conversions—full of charm and character.

At least two houses in the village have the same occupants as in 1914. These are Brook House, owned by Mr. Stokes; and Wilson Cottage, by Mr. and Mrs. Tyler. During the past fifty years about forty-five houses and bungalows have been built by the council in the main village. Although *all* " mod cons." cannot yet be a local advertising point, a main water supply became available in 1940 and electricity soon after. Before the water was laid on, the pump on the green served the residents at the top of the hill and a stream supplied those at the bottom. The excellent water drawn from the spring by the brook has been piped by the council, and its mineral virtues, according to those who regularly use it, are well worth the trouble of going daily to fetch it. The old-fashioned yoke with a pail at each end is still used.

For the crowning amenity, modern sanitation, the village waits with monumental patience and reasonable hope.

CHAPTER 2

PLACES OF WORSHIP

BEFORE the building of the parish church in 1870 the spiritual needs of the villagers were not disregarded, but the vicar of the parent parish of Great Waltham, even with the assistance of a curate, must have found it an intolerably large area to serve conscientiously. Services then were held in the large barn at Hill Farm, which is known to this day as Vestry Barn.

The foundation stone of the parish church, on the exterior east wall, states " . . . the church of Fourth End, Great Waltham, was laid . . . by Eleanor Margaret, wife of John Jolliffe Tufnell, of Langleys, Esquire, on 23rd May, 1870." The church, erected by subscription, was consecrated in 1871 and the register dates from that year. Its architect was Frederick Chancellor; its style early English, with polygonal apse. The spired tower is adorned by large figures of the evangelists. The south aisle is covered by the same big roof span as the nave, giving low, one-light south aisle windows. The timbered porch does not follow medieval precedent. Two of the six bells were added in 1881, and another in 1893, when the chancel was rebuilt and a new organ chamber erected on the north side at a cost of £600 by the Rev. H. E. Hulton, vicar of Great Waltham.

Features of outstanding merit are the fine pulpit, lectern and choir stalls in dark oak, designed and magnificently carved by Col. Nevill Tufnell, of Langleys. It is grievous that these fine carvings have suffered the ravages of woodworm. Perhaps the surpassing beauty of such craftsmanship is in danger of being underestimated by this generation, which tends to take the riches of the past too lightly, seeing with the unseeing eye of familiarity.

On entering the church attention is readily focused on the beautifully painted three-panel reredos, centrally depicting the crucified Christ, flanked by the figures of St. Mary and St. John. The figures appear in striking relief against the Mediterranean-blue background. The painting was recently cleaned and restored by an artist of the Wareham Guild as a memorial to a former parishioner, the late Mr. Leslie D. Clarke.

The first incumbent was the Rev. Francis Yolland, whose vicariate extended from 1870 to 1886. His successors are:

The Rev. John Littlewood	1888—1891
,, ,, Allan Armitage	1892—1894
,, ,, Arthur S. Cripps	1895—1900
,, ,, R. D. Grindley	1901—1904
,, ,, R. S. Dewing	1905—1909
,, ,, W. S. Hatch	Jan.—Aug. 1910
,, ,, Francis Nicholson	1910—1917
,, ,, Charles Heaslop	1918—1919
,, ,, John Lewis Evans	1919—1926
,, ,, Arthur S. Cripps	1927—1930
,, ,, Leonard S. Wilson	1930—1932
,, ,, R. F. Dawson	1933—1942
,, ,, Edward Grant	1942—1945
,, ,, James C. Morrice	1946—1947
,, ,, Reginald W. Eastment ..	1947—1961
,, ,, P. E. James	1962—1964
,, ,, H. J. C. Hughes	1964—1966
,, ,, B. W. Jukes (priest-in-charge)	1966—

The parish registers provide an interesting study. Not a few parishioners in earlier days signed with a X, and family names occur at almost rhythmic intervals, to the second, third and even fourth generations. The marriage register records the fact that " J. Joyce, being a ringer, the bells

Parish church—east end.

The Mill House, Hartford End.

Hartford End mill.

Above : Black Chapel.

Right : the Cripps memorial.

The Vicarage.

The parish church (St. John the Evangelist).

were rung for the first time on the *occasion of a wedding*, on 26th May, 1883 "—Mr. Joyce being the happy bridegroom.

The church—impressively light and clean—has the added attraction of a scrupulously tidy churchyard, with two broad expanses of neat turf, each planted with a splendid rose bed in proportionate size.

Behind the church is the vicarage, in a pretty, spacious garden. The house is large and attractive, in red brick, with gabled roof. But for the intolerable problem of upkeep it could justly be termed a " highly desirable residence." Both vicarage and church have been underpinned, the subsidence in each case being attributed to unsuitable subsoil—former osier beds. But popular legend maintains that they were built on " stolen ground "—so what could you expect?

The gift of the living is in the hands of Trinity College, Oxford.

Black Chapel, a small chapel of ease at North End, on the Dunmow road, is a feature of outstanding historical interest, dating from about 1500, when it was a monastery chapel, though in its form—half tenement, half church—it bears little resemblance to conventional church architecture. Its name suggests that Augustinian monks sang masses there in olden days.The services held at Black Chapel are according to the rite of the Church of England, but it is a " peculiar," that is outside the jurisdiction of the bishop of the diocese; and by a strange anomaly the incumbent of the parish has no say in the administration of its affairs although he has the pastoral care of those who reside in the area and worship there. By designation the incumbent is " vicar of Ford End with Black Chapel "; he celebrates the Holy Communion there every month and at festivals and, in turn with two other priests, officiates at evensong on Sundays, but Black Chapel is administered by trustees and the incumbent is not one of them. He receives a fee from the trustees for his services. It is a quaint little building, described in *The People's History of Essex* as " unromantic," but it has the engaging charm of age and atmosphere. The chancel shows the older pews and the later horse-box pews beneath the double-decker pulpit. There is a musicians' gallery, containing a barrel-organ which is no longer used. Above the screen hangs a painting of the royal arms, with A and R at the top corners and the date of Queen Anne's death at the bottom. This is said to have been carried into the open on the decease of every subsequent ruler of the realm. Black Chapel is not licensed for weddings and the surrounding ground has not been consecrated, so burials cannot take place there; but baptisms are permissible. The font, like everything else about Black Chapel, is unusual. It is probably the smallest stone font in existence.

Black Chapel was endowed by Ann Wiseman, of North End, in 1681, and in accordance with her will the sum of " three-score pounds " was paid into the hands of six of the chief inhabitants, " in trust to purchase lands . . . the rents and profits . . . to be laid out for the maintenance of an honest and orthodox minister, to preach every Sunday in the Chapel of North End "; but in the event of North End being " unprovided of a minister " the said rents were to be distributed among the local poor, according to specific instructions. The abstract quoted was taken from a recital in an indenture, dated February 14, 1835, purporting to be a conveyance of the premises purchased under the will to new trustees. The " three-score pounds " was " laid out in the purchase of a messuage in the parish, now the public-house called the Butcher's Arms, and of two acres of arable land, let to William Snow on lease for ten years from Michaelmas 1835."

The character and terms of numerous parochial charities shed a penetrating light on the social history of the times; for example " three barrels of white, and one and a half barrels of red herrings, in Lent," from Lord Rich's charity, and £5/4/- left by J. Shuttleworth, in 1723, " out of Graveley's, to be given 2/- weekly, in bread, to twelve widows," etc., but the literal administration of such charities today presents an insoluble problem. The " herring " charity, for instance, was subsequently converted into calico, commonly known as the " Herring Gift Calico." Those entitled to benefit received six yards of unbleached calico once in three or four years. As the price of calico rocketed small monetary allocations were substituted.

Zoar Chapel. Congregationalism was well established in the village towards the middle of the nineteenth century; in fact Zoar Chapel was built by an ancestor of Mr. J. J. Tufnell, of Langleys, in 1844 (twenty-six years before the parish church). Today there is a non-resident lay pastor in charge, but formerly Zoar had a resident minister, whose manse was the small red-brick cottage at the top of the hill. In the capacity of lay pastor the late Mr. R. Loft, of Shirleys, will be long remembered. He and Mrs. Loft gave years of unstinted service to Zoar. Advanced age and infirmity compelled Mr. Loft finally to relinquish leadership to a younger man, and Mr. Theo C. Brown was inducted at an impressive recognition service in June 1956.

The Anglican mission church of the Good Shepherd, Littley Green, was built in 1896, during the earlier vicariate of the Rev. A. Shearley Cripps. The mission church is a simple little wooden structure on land belonging formerly to Graveley's Farm. Through the past sixty years it has served the parishioners in that remote and rather inaccessible area, which to this day lacks transport facilities. As there is no assistant curate, the vicar of Ford End attends the mission one Sunday each month to celebrate Holy Communion and to officiate at evensong, and, of course, at all festivals. For years to come the names of Crozier, Thurgood and Davies will be affectionately remembered for their faithful allegiance to the mission church; and more recently Mrs. J. W. Gardner started a morning Sunday school for the Littley Green children, with really encouraging prospects. In 1956, to mark the diamond jubilee of the mission church, the interior was redecorated, a pleasing cream paint replacing the sombre dark brown wood, and a new dorsal and altar furnishings were acquired, mainly through a legacy from the late Mrs. Felix Crozier. The actual work was undertaken by members of the congregation as an act of devoted service. The new altar frontal and hangings were blessed by the Rev. Ralph Bell, C.R., who was at the time conducting an evangelistic mission in Ford End.

The Ark. Of the Ark there remains no structural evidence today. It was demolished in 1954 after standing empty and desolate for some years and becoming utterly derelict. It was a small ark-shaped building in the garden of the cottage recently renamed Little Owls (which, incidentally, is probably the oldest house in Ford End). It was used as a Strict Baptist chapel, and in its time was well attended, worshippers coming in some cases long distances, bringing food with them for the day. Since its closure around 1925 Baptists have had no local organization.

CHAPTER 3

SCHOOLS

EDUCATION in the village has made impressive strides from the days when rudimentary instruction in the three Rs was given by Mrs. Anna M. Joyce in the little " school " held at the Spreadeagle inn and later at the Old School House (more accurately bungalow!), close by the brook, to the present day, when the local mixed primary school, under the Essex education authority, feeds the neighbouring grammar and secondary modern schools with the local eleven-pluses. The actual date of the Spreadeagle seat of learning is somewhat obscure, but by reasonable deduction it must have existed around 1850 to 1870, the most reliable clue being that Mrs. Emma Harman, who died in 1955 at the age of ninety-two, and was a granddaughter of Mrs. Joyce the school dame, was the last pupil to be accepted at the Spreadeagle " school." The mistress used the old-fashioned horn book for teaching the alphabetical elements of reading, and Mrs. Harman treasured to the day of her death her own horn-book primer. Parents had to pay a few coppers a week for their children's education.

North End in the old days had its own primitive educational facilities. Lessons were given at Black Chapel schoolroom under the instruction of a Mrs. Fowler. From documents in the Essex Record Office it is authoritatively learnt that " out of the rents [from specified charities] there is paid . . . £3 yearly to Mrs. Fowler for teaching the 30 children hereafter mentioned at the Sunday-school . . . both girls and boys; no distinction is made as to sect. The children attend the chapel on Sunday. They are taught the catechism, and to read; but not to write. Some of the children attend Mrs. Fowler also on weekdays, for which the parents pay a small sum." Also in North End a Miss Auger instructed a few pupils in a tiny cottage in the lane approaching North End Place.

A small private school was also conducted by a Miss Young at King's Farm, owned by her father, a veterinary surgeon.

The present school—at least one room of it—was built in 1869. It was the private property of Mr. J. J. Tufnell, was managed by the vicar (B. S. Yolland), and was used also for a Sunday school. The annual income was £16 (£6 voluntary contributions and £10 school pence), with an average attendance of thirty-eight. In 1873 it was extended to its present (1958) proportions, with teachers' residence. Weekly payments were 2d., and 1d. for each additional child from the same family. The first certificated teacher was Leslie C. Evans, appointed in 1874 at a salary of £80 per annum. In 1950 the school became a Church of England primary controlled school and the over-elevens were transferred to Rainsford Road, Chelmsford.

Today, when the principles of education are more rigorously applied, evidence of the rather haphazard methods of the 1870s strikes an amusing note. According to the first school log book, lessons were of secondary importance in a locality where the urgency of field work went unchallenged. Contemporary social conditions are reflected in such extracts as:

> " 1874. March 7th. Several children away bird-scaring. The treasurer informs me that he has no funds and he will not be able to pay my stipend or the pupil teacher's after this month. The ground on which this school stands has never been conveyed; because of this and an objection to the Constitution, the Trustees inform me officially that they resign and close the school after this month.

" March 27th. Difficulty as to school funds removed by voluntary rate.

" April 20th. The National Society have voted £10 towards my stipend.

" May 8th, 15th, 22nd. Absence as children away osier-peeling.

" June 26th. Children away pea-picking.

" July 30th. Broke up. Harvest holiday 5 weeks.

" September 18th. Attendance small. Harvest protracted on account of wet weather.

" November 20th. Teacher left. School closed till February 27th.

" 1875. February 27th. Attendance very small, as not generally known that school had reopened.

" March 25th. Some boys away at work in fields against law (Agricultural Act).

" November 6th. Bad attendance—some children working in the fields, others gathering acorns.

" 1876. March 31st. Children away bird-scaring. Half-holiday to enable children to go to Hunt.

" May 22nd. First day of new scale of fees. Several boys brought old fees. Sent home for remainder. Did not return that day.

" 1877. May 10th. Several boys expressed a desire to learn art. Allowed them half an hour for that.

" October 12th. Several between 7 and 9 do not even know alphabet.

The log book continues in this vein, with attendance conditioned by seasonal bird-scaring, osier-peeling, pea-picking, hay-making, harvesting, gleaning, and weather—many scholars having long distances to walk to school. The normal complement on the staff consisted of one teacher, a pupil teacher and a monitor. The monitor was recruited from the older pupils, but candidates for pupil teacher had to pass an examination.

CHAPTER 4

SHOPS

THE terse caption " shops " may tend to create a mental picture of a row of neat, enterprising little stores competing briskly for the village patronage, whereas in fact there has seldom been more than one such business, or at the most two, running at one time. But over the years there has been a surprising succession of traders. Naturally, in the days when transport facilities were poor or non-existent villagers had to rely almost entirely on the local butcher, baker and candlestick maker.

Today (1958) the village is served by the local branch of the Cambridge Co-operative Society, whose miscellaneous stock—from gum-boots to paraffin, bread to shaving cream—seems to meet most household wants, and this source is supplemented by Mrs. Goad's recently established store at the new post office. These two have no other trading rivals today.

The Co-op, however, is successor to the Ford End Village Stores opened originally by a Mr. Baker. He was followed by Mr. Robert Brown, who carried on a very flourishing business there. For many years, in fact, this was the only shop, supplying almost every conceivable household commodity. Four bakers were employed and their excellent bread earned a reputation as far afield as Springfield, daily deliveries being made by horse and van. Besides groceries Mr. Brown sold drapery, men's wear, boots and shoes, and coal. Post office transactions were also conducted in this shop until the Co-op took over. For some years there was no post office in the village for want of accommodation.

At one time the Swan Stores was run by Mr. Alfred Smith, and more recently Mrs. Hawkes's little grocery shop at the top of the hill was a real boon to those in the immediate vicinity. Not a few nearby customers sighed regretfully when this business closed down.

Older residents remember a shoemaker's shop-cum-post-office run by a Mr. Charlie Fowler in part of the cottages known as Cambrai. The post office was previously at Shirleys. Not a hundred yards away—in fact next door to Zoar—Mr. Thomas Coe (once mine host at the Swan) demonstrated his business acumen in the multiple rôle of carpenter, painter, baker and undertaker—a strange combination if ever there was one! It was jokingly said of him that he was not content to make a living out of the public while they were alive, so he made a bit more from them after they were dead.

The weatherboarded cottage in The Chase, owned today by Mr. and Mrs. J. Wilks, was once an off-licence called The Harrows.

In the days of horse-drawn vehicles there was ample scope in any village for a wheelwright, and Ford End's Mr. Jim Coe usefully filled this rôle at the premises now called The Laurels. The actual shop was at the rear and was finally demolished about 1925, although the business had ceased around 1905. Mr. Coe had a successor in Mr. Jim Root.

The name of Coe crops up frequently in the village records, and it was a Mr. Amos Coe who was the village blacksmith. The old smithy stood where today is the delightful garden attached to Shirleys. The business later passed to Mr. Davey, but in 1913 a disastrous fire totally destroyed the premises. This calamity, which occurred during a church service, constituted a major sensation in the village, not alone because of the awesome sight of the blazing smithy, but equally because of the dramatic interruption of the service as a certain Mrs. Lodge—the blacksmith's neighbour—rushed frantically into church shouting "Come quick; come quick! We shall all be burnt up in our beds." Her grim prophecy was unfounded, but Ford End lost its smithy, despite all heroic efforts to control the blaze with buckets of water from the stream. Incidentally, this was not the only memorable conflagration in Ford End; three houses were destroyed by fire at Ringtail Green, one at Cobben Docks, another at Porters, Hall and Mr. Cass's former house at Appletrees.

Pursuing the business thread, "Fishy" Reeves is remembered for his enterprising little stores in the house called Greys, owned now by the Bartrupt family.

North End had its own shopping facilities, albeit on somewhat Lilliputian lines. The "shop" was in the back room at the old Black Chapel Cottage (so recently and attractively modernized by Mr. Lanes). Here was Fowler's Provision Stores. Then close to North End green was Thomas Smith—General Stores, with adjacent nursery garden. The son, Owen Smith, was a familiar figure, carrying the produce in a basket on his head to the neighbouring villages.

The parish has not always been without a butcher, and the delicious sausages for which Mr. William Snow (better known as "Scudby") was famed seem to this day to arouse nostalgic longings in some of the older inhabitants. His pork butcher's shop was at The Chestnuts, North End, close to the Butcher's Arms. He covered an extensive round on foot, carrying two large baskets, as far away as Felsted, Little Dunmow and Great Dunmow. Oak Cottage was once the Oaks public-house.

Today local housewives are obligingly "waited upon" by tradesmen from the surrounding areas—Braintree, Felsted, Dunmow and Great Waltham. For the rest there is the weekly trek to Chelmsford, where Friday's market seems to provide a magnetic pull.

It is but a slight, and perhaps natural, deviation from "shops" to "other industries," among which Ridley's brewery and mill at Hartford End claim a prominent place. In former days the mill made the stone-ground flour for bakers and housewives, and provided corn-grinding services to the farmers. Before motor transport the beer was distributed by three-horse drays, and about twenty-five horses were kept at the brewery for the purpose. Deliveries were made as far afield as Saffron Walden, Barking and Southminster, and a ripe story persists locally of a drayman who fell asleep coming down Littley Park Avenue. The horses went over the bridge at the foot and the whole contraption overturned into a ditch, rudely shattering the driver's nap! Unhappily, one horse broke its neck and one had to be shot. The brewery, although regarded as a local industry and employing village labour, is not strictly within the parish. It is over the Felsted boundary.

The thatcher's art is seen to great advantage in the village, and the Stokes family, of Brook House, for three generations (from approximately 1850) have been expert thatchers. First there was William Stokes (known as "Brookie"), then his son, George, then Sidney. By coincidence, there was another thatcher named Ben Stokes, but he was of a different family and was also a maker of wooden hurdles.

The local threshing industry, for which the Bartrupt family has built up a wide reputation, was associated in the first instance with the name of Millbank at North End and later with that of Armstrong at Hill Farm, but it will certainly be with the name of Bartrupt that future generations will associate the spectacular growth of the threshing industry in these parts—beginning with a horse-drawn portable machine, then progressing to steam and finally to diesel-driven plant.

The following are the farms which today provide the main agricultural labour.

Poulters, owned and farmed by Mr. V. C. Britton in succession to his uncle, Mr. Fred Britton, and grandfather, Mr. Josiah Britton.

Hill Farm, which passed from Mr. Armstrong to Mr. William Matthams, then to Mr. Charles Britton, and now to Mr. Leonard Bartrupt.

Lavenders. This farm was sold fifty-one years ago by Mr. Philip Dowsett to Mr. W. B. Smith, who farmed there until his retirement in 1950, when it was bought by Mrs. Freeman.

The Wall. A succession of tenant farmers has cultivated The Wall. Within relatively recent times it was farmed by Mr. William Hasler, later by Mr. E. G. Row, then by Mr. V. C. Britton until his move to Poulters in 1938, when Mr. G. S. White became farmer at The Wall.

Kings was owned and farmed for many years by Mr. Fred Young, who also acquired fame as a veterinary surgeon and was an outstanding character among his contemporaries. His son, Solomon, followed the father's profession, practising at Coggeshall. For a short while Mr. Moore farmed at Kings, but it is now owned by Mr. B. Marven, fruit farmer, who bought the property in 1949.

Littley Park was formerly owned and farmed by Mr. Harry Wood, who was succeeded by his son, Mr. R. Praed Wood.

In every village family groups become vigorously rooted and, over the years, extend their branches in ever-broadening growth, generation after generation. Reflecting this pattern of development, certain surnames crop up in epidemic proportions, and with Ford End the names of Bartrupt, Britton, Stokes, Perkins, Hornsby and Burr—to mention only a few—have been associated for a century and are not likely to fade out.

CHAPTER 5

PERSONALITIES

WITH such a rich galaxy of local characters to claim attention the problem of selection cannot be evaded. To refer once more to Mr. Fred Young, vet-cum-farmer, although he ceased to practise as a veterinary surgeon some years before the 1930s his vital personality has left an impression that time will not easily destroy. He was a popular, respected figure, always driving on his rounds in a gig.

Mr. Thurgood, miller, of Hartford End, is remembered not only as a chorister for sixty years and a much-respected parishioner, but also—though less generally perhaps—for the episode of the pork pie hat. He always attended church wearing a pork pie hat. Once when walking through Littley Park he stopped to admire Kitty, the old mare. Kitty, with scandalous irreverence, whipped off his hat. On the return journey Mr. Thurgood paused again, admonishing Kitty with " You *wicked* old mare," whereupon she seized his hat again and bit it clean in half.

The Copeland family occupies almost an entire wall of the local picture gallery. Mr. Copeland was the headmaster who preceded Mr. Franklin, and his was clearly a scholarly family, for his two sons, Willie and George, and his daughter, Nellie, all taught in the school; and George added further lustre to the family reputation as church organist.

Of all the local characters few seem to have enjoyed greater popularity than Mr. Henry Franklin, schoolmaster, who took over from the Copeland family around 1892 and held office for about twenty years. The affectionate nickname Daddy Franklin persists to this day. He was a keen sportsman, upright and sturdy of build, and a great walker. Above all, he was a strict disciplinarian, and many are the tales of boys returning home ruefully holding the seats of their knicker-bockers, having tasted a few sharp raps from Daddy's cane, which lived in warning prominence on the top of his desk. His popularity was not diminished by his strictness. He had an immense keenness for the Navy and often took parties of village lads to Portsmouth on day outings to see the ships. These excursions began at 3 a.m., the journey being made by horse and cart to Chelmsford and thence by train, the party returning by 3 o'clock the following morning. Once Daddy's son scored a century for Essex, which illustrious performance earned the local school a day's holiday. From Ford End school Mr. Franklin went to Great Waltham, and he now lives in retirement at Willingdale.

Another weathered character of earlier days was the local carrier, Jim Cheek, who, with his familiar black mare, plied between Chelmsford and surrounding districts. He was successor to Charlie Fowler. Besides carrying, Jim Cheek undertook shoe-mending (at the Spreadeagle), and is also said to have contrived a bit of farming, He made the journey twice weekly to Chelmsford—on Mondays and Fridays. Anyone wanting a lift to "town" was lucky to get a seat on top of the boxes loaded on to his open cart, or perhaps the tailboard would be lowered for extra accommodation, and for the privilege of this comfortless ride the charge was 8d. return. Mr. Cheek, by the way, was also church clerk, an office now defunct.

Apparently a little harmless competition later developed in the carrying business, for the names of Quiff Reeve and E. Coe are also recalled in this connection.

A position of special prominence in the gallery of local

personalities must be reserved for the Rev. Arthur Shearly Cripps, twice vicar of Ford End, with an intervening period of service in the African mission field. The mention of Mr. Cripps (uncle of the famous austerity Chancellor of the Labour Government) invariably inspires the wistful comment " Of course *he* was a perfect saint," implying a degree of other-worldliness to which ordinary mortals can never reasonably hope to attain. A graduate of Trinity College, Oxford, he was a man of scholarly attainments and an author and poet of real merit. He was also a keen sportsman and athlete, having won his half blue for boxing and rowing. Locally he is remembered as a sprinter capable of outstripping any likely opponent, and he was seldom seen to walk where he could possibly run. He never spared himself in any way, and has been known literally to give away the shoes off his feet, and on more than one occasion to take out his own dinner to a hungry vagrant. He was a splendid organizer; a man of deep compassion and of almost monastic frugality in his personal tastes. While preferring for himself private lodgings at Brook House, the vicarage was given over for recreational uses, and a soup kitchen for poor children was available there. Coming to Ford End as a young man in 1894, his energies were soon engaged in forming a football club. He revived the picturesque traditional maypole dancing, and through his efforts the annual village sports became a feature. On November 5 each year he would organize a torchlight procession, and the village bonfire ritual became firmly established. Mr. Cripps also organized frequent village socials, making persuasive demands upon local talent. With a shrewd eye to the ethics of humanitarianism, he started for the children a " Band of Mercy," in conjunction with which a pets' show was held annually, and the care of dumb animals became a matter of real concern among the youngsters. The parish church has been immortalized in his poem " Essex ";

musing reflectively on the natural enchantment of the river scene, Mr. Cripps identifies the

" Chelmer whose mill and willows
Keep one red tower in sight "

—the bold tower of Ford End's parish church.

Long as Mr. Cripps will be remembered as a compassionate parish priest, it is through his zeal for evangelism in the mission field, which drew him back to Enkeldoorn, Southern Rhodesia, after his second vicariate at Ford End, that he will go down to posterity. He died among his beloved natives, in Enkeldoorn hospital, in August 1952 at the age of eighty-three, blind, but cared for by the natives to whom he had ministered with such devotion and had finally given all his property to the point of complete poverty.

An example of beautiful symbolic carving—in the native African tradition—was presented to the parish church by the diocese of Mashonaland in memory of Mr. Cripps and as a mark of appreciation of his tireless work among the coloured Africans. It was dedicated in August 1960 by Canon R. G. Gibbon, rector of Borrowdale, Salisbury, Southern Rhodesia, acting for the Bishop of Mashonaland. This pleasing gesture will be a permanent reminder to the parishioners of Ford End of their former vicar's unremitting concern for the work of evangelism in the mission field and his deep compassion for his underprivileged brothers.

Another poet of distinction who lived at North End and worshipped regularly at Black Chapel was Ruth Pitter, who made her cultural mark in 1937, when she joined the select ranks of Hawthornden prizewinners for the best imaginative literature published during the previous twelve months. " One of the most distinguished of living writers " was Lord David Cecil's estimate of her in his 1951 review of her published selection, " Urania." For her work " The Ermine " Ruth Pitter received one of the two Heinemann

Black Chapel.

Littley Park—a gem of an Essex farmhouse.

Foundation awards for 1953, but her special recognition came in 1955, when the court circular from Buckingham Palace disclosed that " Miss Ruth Pitter had the honour of being received by the Queen, when Her Majesty presented to her the Queen's gold medal for poetry for 1955." Normally the prize is presented by the Poet Laureate, but Miss Pitter, being the first woman to receive the award, was called to Buckingham Palace, where fifteen minutes alone with Her Majesty must have seemed worth many gold medals! Poets no doubt have a limited following, but Miss Pitter's public can safely be counted in millions now that she has been recruited to the B.B.C. television Brains Trust, and as a radio broadcaster she has an established reputation.

Living with Miss Pitter at North End was her sister, Shirley Murrell, novelist, with a preference for historic themes, whose literary output is as stimulating as it is prolific. Miss Murrell's first novel, *Perilous Rock*, published in 1948 (Hodder and Stoughton), which tells of Winstanley's supremely brave but tragic enterprise in the design and construction of the first Eddystone lighthouse, was followed by a steady stream of stirring tales, each based on historical fact but presented in the captivating style of a vivacious narrator. In private life Shirley Murrell is remembered in Ford End as Mrs. Olive Scott-Hansen.

Another local medallist, in a totally different sphere, was Mr. William Joyce—"Bill" to all and sundry. He was employed by Mr. Fred Britton, and he was an acknowledged character in the pea fields, where his subtle genius as a " tier " made him in great demand. He received the gold medal for long service—sixty years on one farm—from the hands of King George VI at the county agricultural show at Orsett.

In our own day Miss Dorothy Jean Britton, of Poulter's Farm, has made a handsome contribution to village fame as an outstanding lacrosse player, reaching international status by representing England on many occasions, including a tour of the United States.

Some of the local comics, who gave generously of their varying talents and left imperishable memories behind, surely deserve a mention among the " personalities." When village communities were more completely cut off from the outside world entertainment was necessarily home-brewed —a factor which disclosed a degree of hidden ability in many a shy and trembling breast. There are stories galore of village concerts in the best possible tradition—rollicking songs, rousing choruses, wild applause, and musical reputations established with meteoric suddenness. Some of the old songsters did their turns in the pubs, stimulated no doubt by the convivial atmosphere and attendant " spirits." Mr. Jack Brown, of Ringtail Green, immortalized " So to Chelmsford they went through the air " (a queer title, rather suggesting local authorship). Mr. David Collins is reputed to have been able to sing only with his eyes closed, and his favourite " O pray, young shepherd, will you come home? " was given with such monotonous regularity that on one occasion when he opened his eyes at the final note the audience had fled and he found himself alone in the empty hall.

A certain Mr. George Everitt, familiarly known as Tom Gafney, seldom failed to oblige with " Kitty Wells," a gloomy ballad whose chorus ended on the mournful line " That's when we laid her in the tomb." Mr. Walter Hawkes is best remembered for his armchair ditties, Mr. Alfred Linge for his stirring number " The dark-eyed sailor " and Mr. George " Ninety " Joyce for " The old carrion crow." Other now-neglected ditties such as " I'm a city swell," "Hearts of oak" and "O where is that hat?" all had their robust interpreters in Messrs. Fred Coe, George Collins and Edward Wallis; but Mr. William Barker was almost ahead of his time with " She lost her situation through the great big wheel " and " I drive the bus that many rides on."

In the more sober climate of the schoolroom, where so many of the concerts were held, Teddy Lawn, Jack Sides and Harry Wood were among the talented amateurs who, with their comic songs and a piano, drew good audiences. It is rumoured that all present drank beer from stone flagons smuggled into the back of the schoolroom—to stimulate and sustain!

CHAPTER 6

ACTIVITIES AND CUSTOMS

A SAD reflection on village life in most counties is the decline in the social and cultural activities of a generation ago—despite the Women's Institutes' determined policy to stop the rot. Cheap cars, the weekend habit and television provide the clue. Ford End is no exception. Many cultural endeavours got off to a good start and initial support kept them happily afloat long enough for agreeable memories to have been registered. A typical example was the Ford End and District Choral Society, formed in 1913 by Mr. Archibald Bullock, headmaster of that day. He assembled an impressive choir, sixty strong, whose ambitions apparently knew no limit, for they managed to give a full performance of Handel's " Messiah " with the able assistance of professionals from London for the solo parts—an achievement talked of to this day with immeasurable pride. The performance was given in the school, as were most events until the village hall was built in 1922. The local reputation circulated, and invitations came for repeat renderings in neighbouring villages. The musical tradition is maintained today by the church choir, but there is no secular group to carry on Mr. Bullock's good work on the more ambitious scale.

North End once had its own brass band, under the tuition of a Mr. Owen Smith (not to be confused with the Owen Smith already referred to).

Shortly after World War II an amateur dramatic group was formed. If less ambitious than the choral society it was every bit as enthusiastic. It gave a few memorable shows and deserved a better fate than the early dissolution that awaited it for lack of public support.

A consistently gratifying record is held by the Women's Institute, founded in May 1919 and still flourishing vigorously (1958). It has undoubtedly been of immense value, not only in fostering the spirit of friendly co-operation among its members but in stimulating locally a lively concern for matters of general interest and importance far beyond the boundaries of village life, replacing a narrowly parochial outlook with a vision of affairs on a national and international level, and making available to village dwellers facilities for expert instruction in all the domestic arts and crafts. The general standard of homecraft reflects splendid efficiency today. The " know-how " is now the common property of all local housewives; not, as formerly, of just those fortunate few who could afford to pay for expensive, specialized tuition. The subjects of instruction in those early days followed a more severely practical pattern, and none perhaps was more practical than the cobbling class held in 1919, which was eagerly supported. By comparison, some of the more delicate and elaborate subjects so popular today seem almost frivolous. Naturally, competitions in those days reflected the practical trend; for instance, one contest in 1925 was for " the best patched pair of boots," and the second prizewinner on that occasion was Mrs. Wren, still an active parishioner. The present membership also includes two other founder members: Mrs. W. B. Smith and Mrs. Nathan Tyler. The Women's Institute, in common with other organizations in the pre-hall days, met at the clubroom, the large side room at Hill Farm Cottage, next to the vicarage—welcome accommodation indeed in a village that had neither church hall nor community centre.

Over the years the women parishioners have responded well to organized efforts to maintain and extend the interests of their church. At one time an industrious little band of women, known appropriately as the Willing Workers, used to meet regularly to repair the church linen and to keep the cassocks, surplices and kneelers in good condition. Later on, as members of the Mothers' Union, they became a valuable ancillary body to the church both in witness and in action, always ready to put a willing shoulder to the parochial wheel whatever the project in hand. Eventually the Churchwomen's Guild evolved from these earlier groups to keep the torch of faith and fellowship burning, to the certain enrichment of the community.

Mrs. Dawson inaugurated a branch of the Girls' Friendly Society, which had an uneventful, brief existence.

The British Legion, with its complementary women's section, started after World War I, and although it seems to attract little new support there remains a hard core of faithful members to uphold its splendid tradition.

In a wide variety of ways the young people of the village have been catered for through the years, and the extent to which provision for the younger generation seems to be lacking today reflects not failure to recognize their needs but, for the most part, the difficulty encountered nearly everywhere of finding leaders to undertake the work. The present incumbent (the Rev. R. W. Eastment) was instrumental in forming troops of Scouts, Guides, Cubs and Brownies, but as one leader after another, for private or business reasons, had to relinquish responsibility the intractable problem of replacement manifested itself. Similarly with the Youth Fellowship, inaugurated in 1947 by the present vicar as an " open " organization for the young people of the village, the problem of high spirits and spasmodic attendance, combined with the perennial problem of finding new leaders, accounted for its untimely discontinuance after seven years of laborious striving. All likely tastes were catered for; on the sports side there were facilities for table tennis, darts, chess, card games, and occasional hiking expeditions in the summer. On the cultural side the programmes included lectures and discussions, film shows, dramatic recitals and musical evenings in the vicarage drawing room, when professional London musicians gave their services. Of the recitalists, Miss Fay Middleton and Mr. Frank Johnson—both eminent authorities on Dickens—gave unforgettable evenings of character sketches from their Dickensian repertoires; and on several occasions Mr. Basil Wright, one of the pioneers in this country of documentary film production (and incidentally a familiar figure on the radio as chairman of "The Critics"), gave delightful film shows, with explanatory talks on the intricacies of film shooting and sound production. It is greatly to be hoped that a revival of the Youth Fellowship may not be long delayed. Funds and equipment await the moment when new leaders shall be forthcoming.

The youngest parish group, now in its second year, is the Women's Fellowship, which, by offering the hand of friendship and the occasion for pleasant social relaxation, caters primarily for the younger married women—while fathers baby-sit. The fellowship bids fair to become a strong force in the parish. The moving spirit behind its inauguration was Mrs. Joan Clarke, whose home—Redes—provides the meeting place.

The Garden Association is the organization which tends gracefully to efface itself for the greater part of the year but comes convincingly into its own at the annual summer show, when the display of local garden wizardry never fails to evoke the judges' highest praise. The outstanding local contestants, like all good gardeners, seem to meet the challenge of climatic freaks, insect plagues and all other unspecified hazards with imperturbable calm and undiminished skill, invariably timing the perfect exhibit for the right day—but not always, for in 1957 the atrocious weather caused the show to be cancelled for the first time within memory. Mr. Basil Marven, chairman of the association, has done much by way of methodical administration to sustain and foster its growth.

The splendid place that cricket holds in local affection can scarcely be over-estimated and was never, one feels, more clearly demonstrated than when the Rev. R. W. Eastment was about to be instituted to the living in 1947. The ceremony was duly arranged by the bishop of the diocese for a Saturday afternoon in June, but he had to be told, firmly but politely, that it *must* be postponed until 7.30 p.m. to enable the weekly match to take place without let or hindrance. Said the bewildered incumbent-elect to his predecessor, "But the time *can't* be altered; it's been fixed by the *bishop*." The retiring vicar answered, with patient amusement, " It wouldn't matter if it had been fixed by the King himself; your organist is captain; your warden keeps wicket; all your choirmen are in the team; the leader of your choir is scorer; and the rest of the village spectates. So if the bishop doesn't want an entirely empty church he *must* alter it." And he did!

The present club was formed in 1919, and three of the original members are still playing—Messrs. L. Bartrupt, G. Bartrupt and R. Chopping. Three of the members have played since 1927—R. Hornsby, J. Hornsby and R. Theobald. It is no mean record that six members have thus played together for thirty years! By a grievous mishap certain of the club's records were swallowed up overnight, and the villain of the piece was a dog called Cæsar. The bag was packed, with the score book tucked on top, and left overnight at Mr. Hawkes's, whose dog, with a queer taste for statistics or else a spite against the club, seized the book and savagely devoured it, thus depriving posterity of all evidence of the local centuries knocked up that season.

The annual church fête, in the vicarage garden, is an

affair of perennial delight, while the traditional annual outings are a striking feature of local activity—but space forbids detailed mention.

CHAPTER 7

VISITORS

IN the old isolated days the arrival of visitors from the " outside world " always created a pleasant hum of excitement, and not a few of these itinerants—knife-grinders, tinsmiths, chair-menders, cattle drovers, quacks and vets, not to mention members of the gentry journeying forth on their social engagements—left indelible impressions.

Vivid stories are told of the organ-grinder with a monkey which drank beer from a cow's horn and got hilariously drunk. No less colourful are the memories of a well-known cattle drover, Sudbury, who with his collie dog Bess regularly brought cattle through from distant markets, announcing his arrival half a mile off by his lusty halloing and fluent swearing. Two other drovers—Filly Harris and " Ginger," with long red beard and very *lousy*—left a lasting impression, and in the circumstances perhaps more than an impression. In the early 1900s Harry and Charlie Brewer, who hailed from Saffron Walden, were regular figures in charge of cattle, which they drove from Chelmsford market, halting usually for the night at Ford End, where the cattle were pastured on local fields while the drovers slept rough.

It was a common sight about seventy years ago to see a German band pass through the village—about ten in number, blowing and percussing to the limit of human capacity, while the local small fry gathered round in awe and wonder.

An occasion of supreme excitement, if the local reminiscences are to be believed, was the arrival of two Norwegian animal trainers with a couple of performing bears. Who dares to say that the " old days " held no thrills?

Visitations of a more dignified character, but nevertheless causing a considerable stir, were made by the late Countess of Warwick, who frequently drove her four-in-hand from her home at Easton Lodge. It was her custom to stop at King's Farm to change the horses—an entrancing operation to the local youngsters. At least once a year both the Countess of Warwick and Sir Walter Gilbey, of Elsenham Hall, passed through Ford End on their way to the Essex county sports. They each drove a four-in-hand, each using three teams of horses for the journey. The first change would be at the Butcher's Arms, the next at the Angel, Broomfield.

The bustling excitement of a hunt meet—the whole company assembling just by the church—is a pleasantly familiar feature of the local scene.

The first motor-car passed through the village around 1895, and it is not hard to picture the incredulous stares and gasps of wonder that the pioneer motorist must have evoked as he pursued his perilous journey! But the two local pioneers of the new mode of transport were brother farmers—Mr. Charles and Mr. Fred Britton, who owned the first motor-car in Ford End.

Reference to pioneers compels one to mention the first radio set in the village, owned by the schoolmaster, Mr. Griffin, around 1923/4. The schoolchildren were occasionally allowed the unspeakable thrill of listening-in—with headphones, of course. These treats probably constituted one of the first " broadcasts to schools." It is not inappropriate, in the circumstances, that in 1955 Ford End primary school (headmaster, Mr. Howard Slack) should have been chosen by the B.B.C. for the making of a tape-recorded lesson on " How things began," with the children asking questions and Mr. Slack answering and summing up. The purpose of the recording was to help students at teachers' training colleges and conferences.

CHAPTER 7

LOCAL LORE

MUCH as the present generation may deplore the undoubted hardship suffered by the less fortunate villagers in the days before the welfare state, at least the public conscience was alive to the situation, and much was done by individual effort to relieve the heavy burden of poverty, by gifts, thrift clubs and charities. Regrettably, the very word "charity" leaves an unpalatable twang, yet much kindness was dispensed under its label. (Farm wages seventy years ago were under 10/-, remember!)

The church ran a coal club, to which parishioners could pay throughout the year 1/- per month. A shilling bonus was added, and the 13/- bought 13½cwt of coal—which makes one feel that the "old days" were not wholly *bad old days*. No doubt the incredible price was to some extent accounted for by the factor of private transport; local farmers carted it.

The shoe problem, ever acute with children, was catered for by a children's shoe club, the vicar receiving the weekly contributions at the vicarage on Monday mornings. The clothing club also had its business headquarters at the vicarage. By depositing a shilling a month, members could draw out 13/- each November, and then there followed the exciting excursion to Chelmsford to spend the savings on calico, flannel or blankets; and as an extra incentive the draper (Potter's, we are told, was the firm) allowed a special thrift discount of a penny in the shilling.

Further help was available through the Mothers' Meeting, run by Miss Ainger in the old club room. Garments could be bought and paid for at the rate of 6d. per week.

The slender means of those early days encouraged initiative and industry in the home crafts. It was not uncommon for the men to make the baby's pram; there was not the money to buy one. The women used to plait straw for their hats—using plain whipcord and leghorn, all white. The custom was for maids to attend church in uniform, wearing little black bonnets and black or navy coats, or in summer black dresses with white collars and cuffs. The women attended church wearing white aprons and white stockings. If the girls and boys held their first situation twelve months they were given a Bible and ten shillings with which to buy clothes. At Christmas the boys used to be given caps and red comforters, and the girls red capes.

Home baking and brewing were common enough customs, not only for pride in domestic efficiency but also to eke out slender incomes. Improvidence in any shape or form was not only a sin but stark folly. The old people past work and short of means were given the traditional 2/- and a loaf of bread. The precious loaf, if dry, would be dipped in cold water and popped into a hot oven, to emerge crisp and new.

Every village has its legends, superstitions and ghost stories; also its simples. Space permits of only one or two examples, and by coincidence two of Ford End's ghost stories concern animals. One is the ghostly apparition of a white horse which was said to haunt the Rolphy Green area, bobbing up with disconcerting suddenness against the hedges at night to scare the unwary traveller out of his wits. The other is the alleged nerve-shattering appearance of a headless cow, which chose North End for its nocturnal frolics—hence Cowcross Lane!

Despite the claims of modern medical science there are still those in the village who would never deviate from the simple old handed-down remedies; for instance, treatment for a whitlow on the finger is to roll up a piece of dark brown paper and light it so that it smokes. The affected finger must be plunged into the smouldering paper cylinder four times a day. The whitlow, it is claimed, will be gone in six days. The remedy suggests marked courage on the part of the patient and no little skill on the part of the healer to ensure that the smoking paper does not blaze! Again, for ringworm, 1½ ounces of flowers of sulphur mixed with one ounce of pure lard (not shop lard) is rubbed into the affected part. Then a white juice exuded by the stalks of fig leaves is said to be a cure for warts—dabbed on, a drop to a wart. Others pin their faith to the mysterious powers of the wart charmer. The bruised leaves of the foxglove are said to be a remedy for healing open wounds and king's evil; and for a sty simply rub the eye gently several times with a plain gold ring. Orthodoxy would doubtless challenge the efficacy of these homely remedies, but with the nearest doctor five miles distant, and no resident nurse in the parish, local adherence is understandable.

The villagers are accused of taking a too cautious view of newcomers, regarding them as foreigners for at least the first twenty years. One complicated explanation of this phenomenon is that the apparent aloofness is a legacy in perpetuity from the distant days of invasion of our coasts by the Angles, Saxons and Jutes, a situation which constrained the natives to become dumb and suspicious, characteristics they have never lost; but this theory seems too laboured to carry conviction. A more likely explanation is to be found nearer home. About seventy years ago there existed recognized feuds between neighbouring villages, and gang warfare on a minor scale was systematically practised. The people of one village regarded their neighbours over the boundary as foreigners, and natural enemies at that. For instance, it is seriously recorded that if a party of children from Ford End embarked on a trip to Pleshey Mount more often than not they would be chased home by the Pleshey gang, who, not being sufficiently advanced in hooliganism to use coshes, bicycle chains or razors, contented themselves with sticks and stones for weapons. Similarly, if a party of men invaded Ford End for a drink it would assuredly end up in a fight; and no better feeling, it is sad to relate, existed among the womenfolk. Happily these aggressive habits have been abandoned and peace seems to prevail in the countryside; but those bad old days may well account for any reticence even today towards " foreigners."

To do justice to Ford End's war effort—to the spirit of co-operation and loyalty which united all sections against the common enemy, whether in digging for victory, fire-watching, first aid, canning or fruit bottling, making jam in wholesale quantities, engaging in salvage campaigns, receiving evacuees, or actually facing the dangers of service overseas—would need a chronicle on its own and is not, therefore, within the scope of this record. Let it suffice to say that the dignified little war memorial in the churchyard is a permanent reminder of the patriotism that animated the whole community and found expression in service in the hour of peril, and to future generations an eloquent reminder of the immeasurable debt owed to those who secured the freedom of our beautiful countryside at the cost of life itself.

FORD END
VILLAGE HISTORY

Members of the Village History Sub-committee:

Mrs. V. C. Britton
Mrs. Geo. Burr
Mrs. R. Chopping
Mrs. R. Cockrell
Mrs. B. Marven
Mrs. N. Tyler
Mrs. R. W. Eastment

Data, anecdotes and reminiscences contributed by:

Mrs. A. Burr
Mrs. Geo. Burr
Mrs. R. Chopping
Mrs. G. T. James
Mrs. Nightingale
Mrs. J. Rowe
Mrs. W. B. Smith
Mrs. N. Tyler
Mrs. G. S. White
Mrs. John Wood
Mrs. R. W. Eastment
Mr. David Hawkes (per Essex Record Office)

Compiled and written by Winifred V. Eastment